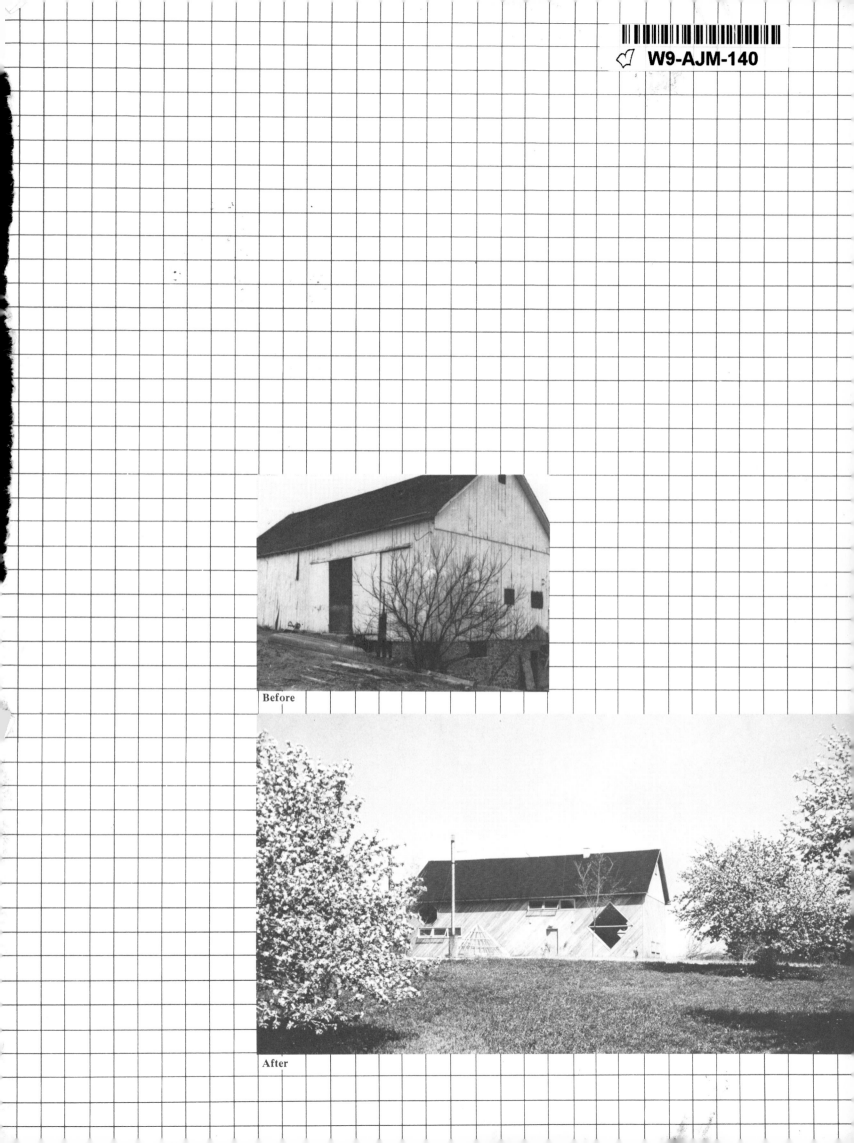

Before

After

**55
REAL-LIFE
CASE
HISTORIES**

HOUSE
& GARDEN'S
BOOK
OF
REMODELING

55
REAL-LIFE
CASE
HISTORIES

A STUDIO BOOK
THE VIKING PRESS
NEW YORK

HOUSE & GARDEN'S BOOK OF REMODELING

This book was planned by
MARY JANE POOL
Editor-in-Chief
HOUSE & GARDEN

Edited by
WILL MEHLHORN
Architecture Editor

Designed by
MIKI DENHOF
Associate Editor

Text written by
BEVERLY RUSSELL
Senior Editor

Copyright © The Condé Nast Publications Inc., 1966, 1968,
1969, 1970, 1971, 1972, 1973, 1974, 1975, 1976, 1978
All rights reserved
First published in 1978 by The Viking Press
625 Madison Avenue, New York, N.Y. 10022
Published simultaneously in Canada by
Penguin Books Canada Limited

Library of Congress Cataloging in Publication Data
Main entry under title:
House & garden's book of remodeling.
  1. Dwellings—Remodeling. I. Pool, Mary Jane.
II. Mehlhorn, Will. III. Russell, Beverly.
IV. House & garden. V. Title: Book of remodeling.
TH4816.H675   728.3   78-18875
ISBN 0-670-37974-3

Printed in the United States of America

Text set in Times Roman; display set in Futura

CONTENTS

INTRODUCTION

Remodeling is a life-sustaining process. One owner who devoted eleven years to reviving an old Pennsylvanian farmhouse said, "There's an intense reward in researching authenticity. When an old house is restored with love and respect for its original architecture, it is enriching to sit in the rooms." For some, there is excitement in responding to the challenge of making over an architectural cinderella. "Great discipline is needed to orchestrate your ideas, so that they harmonize with an existing building," declared an architect who introduced a modern, multi-level living environment into a hundred-year-old barn. Another architect with a skillful knack for pulling an old house gently into the twentieth century admitted that he reveled in "making order out of chaos." There's the satisfaction, too, of watching something grow—like a plant or a child. "The change is a constant source of wonder and pleasure," remarked the couple whose 1845 stone house now boasts a spanking, light-filled modern addition. They rejoice that the familiar living pattern remains—neighbors whose company they enjoy, a community in which they feel comfortable, a garden they've planted and cherished.

We change physically and emotionally, so it is only natural that we want to alter our personal surroundings from time to time. We can satisfy the urge to change by starting out fresh with a new house. Or we can insure a measure of continuity by adding on to or making over what we have. Rather than being uprooted, you find your roots are nourished. The house grows with you, keeping pace with family developments and interests. A new-found need to be more creative may result in a greenhouse kitchen or a garden sewing room. Remodeling extends your individual universe. It opens up a chance for some interesting personal reflection. Questions have to be asked, activities and tastes examined. Very often, this inquiry will redefine who you are. Sometimes it may tell you that you are not the kind of person you thought you were. A gregarious woman with a love of people found herself entranced with the task of organizing a one-room schoolhouse into a weekend retreat that didn't have space for friends to stay. It told her she enjoyed intimacy and a degree of solitude, a small place where two people could enjoy moments of leisure.

Some architectural philosophers believe that not one more new building should be designed before all the existing ones are recycled. Old walls and structures, they explain, are precious character lines on the face of our land. Age must be honored, not cast aside and neglected. This book shows how to go about reviving lofts and barns, old mills and stables, schoolhouses and firehouses, historic houses, row houses and warehouses and odd architectural white elephants—many that initially didn't look as if they had much potential at all.

A psychologist remarked, "Remodeling is a way of achieving self-confidence. It makes you go and do other things—maybe things you didn't feel competent to do before." Such a promise may encourage you to express yourself and taste the exhilaration that results from adding on to or making over *your* space.

1

How to add a
touch of the
Caribbean when
you're living in
Connecticut.

2

Throwing open
the back of a house
to catch a gorgeous
river view.

3

Informalizing a
conventional
Georgian house—
including knocking the
roof out of a
paneled library.

4

Putting a bright,
white, double-decker
surprise on the
back of a prim
Tudor house.

5 6 7 8

:aring down the
rage for a pool,
afting on
v living space.

Adding a five-
room complex
for work and play.

Wrapping a
modern house
around a traditional
stone house.

We have all
had that sur-
prise: sud-
nly discovering one day
at we want to alter the
ouse that once seemed the
rfect place to live. Re-
odeling can be an in-
nsely rewarding experi-
ce. Here are seven smash-
g renovations designed to
tend a house to corre-
ond with developments
 the pattern of family
ing.

WHY NOT ADD ON A NEW WING?

THE SURPRISE OF A CARIBBEAN WING

At first glance, it's a pleasant suburban house, comfortable, friendly, typical. But take a closer look. Advertising executive Folke Lidbeck has added a very private pleasure palace to it and made his house exceptional. The garage, part of a surprising new addition designed by architect Robert Hatch, sits on top of a new game room that doubles as guest space. The real transformation isn't visible until you walk around the house. At the rear, facing a lawn fringed with woods, is a cool Caribbean façade, which admires its own reflection in the swimming pool. Most important—the jewel inside the elegant box —is the new garden room. "We've always loved the islands of the Caribbean," says Babs Lidbeck. "We wanted something that would give us the feeling of being there— relaxed and full of color and light." The arched doorways that echo each other on every side of the room (those on the far wall have bronze mirrored panes) make it a gazebo filled with tropical greenery. Bubble skylights sift light over the jungle. The cool classical parapet around it all encloses a roof patio for sunbathing. The open wing on the right, a skylighted area, holds a marble statue, a tinkling fountain.

The new addition with new front entrance and double garage, 1, was added at left of original gabled house. Slope of land permitted fitting in garden room, 2, at rear on lower level. Garage sits on top of a game room, 3, which serves as guest space and overlooks bocce court, a macadam strip designed for a favorite Italian pastime. Tucked behind the original rear garage, downstairs windows on the left, 4, is a sauna, a souvenir of Mr. Lidbeck's Swedish childhood. Broad brick terraces, 5, surrounding the pool are set with chaise longues and tables reminiscent of the South of France. Counting the Caribbean, the addition includes international references from four nationalities, from places the Lidbecks remember fondly.

10

Life in the new addition is informal, a kind of year-round vacation. "Like being in the Caribbean without having to get there," laughs Mrs. Lidbeck. But it's planned for brisk Connecticut winters, too, to be enjoyed and lived in even when the pool is drained. One of the matching garden-room sofas is covered in white vinyl, to welcome wet bathing suits, but the other is a warm chintz, just as suitable for winter fireplace-watching. The pillows mix. "It looked a little stark the other way." The shiny floor tiles have radiant heat for bare winter-time feet. In summer lunch is often outside, where a locust tree provides cool shade. The terrace has handy access to a small bar off the garden room. Although the addition was made when only one of the three Lidbeck daughters was still at home, the project reflects the Lidbecks' spirited philosophy for years ahead. "We felt the worst thing we could do would be to think of small quarters," says Mr. Lidbeck. "What about grandchildren?" They plan to create an extended family life, with young people in the guest/game room, camping out on the garden-room sofas, sometimes even on the warm floor tiles. The hope is to share activities in the year-long vacation house with as many as possible.

From entrance, 1, stair leads up to glass doors opening on roof deck down to garden room. Overhead is the glass skylight. The orientation of the addition allows little direct sun, but jungle plants thrive under a circular dome in the hallway, 2, which looks like an exhibit in a botanical garden. A hose under the stairway allows watering that doesn't bother the brick floor a bit. The Tavalera tile fountain on the left wall, bought in Spain, sounds like a distant mountain rill. New bar, 3, is useful for entertaining. Main kitchen, 4, got some renovation, too: new cabinets, white sliding doors to closet.

HOUSE-HIGH SCREENED PORCH

Adding a house-high screened porch was the dramatic metamorphosis that gave new life to this intriguing house in Florida. Across the back of the original 1930s structure, architect Jorge Arango spread a graceful cage of plastic screen and black-lacquered steel "to serve as sun protection and a place to enjoy the waterfront view."

It provides a 38-foot-long stone-paved colonnade and plant room. Behind this porch, what had been an awkward sunroom, a roofed terrace, and a second-story porch were converted into full-time rooms, greatly expanding the indoor living space. Downstairs, the sunroom became a general room for family and fun, which joins to the screened porch for parties. The covered terrace was converted to a separate living room for two teen-age daughters. Upstairs, the husband gained a new study, replacing a porch; the wife a bigger bedroom.

"Through simple alterations, the architect provided a new way of living for us," say the Wragges.

Behind the double-height gallery, sliding glass doors on the ground floor lead into new rooms. Family entertaining room, 1, is cooled by overhead fan, needs little care or upkeep. Casual wicker was the choice for furniture, 2, in the daughters' living room. New rooms on the second floor have louvered shutters opening onto the porch. Spare modern look in the upstairs study, 3, with leather chaise. Bedroom extension, 4, becomes a charming sitting room, with cool tiled floor.

BEHIND A GEORGIAN FRONT: FIVE NEW ROOMS

Curving lanes, houses deep-set from the street with broad lawns: the look of this neighborhood in a Southwestern city is a mixture of red-brick Georgian fronts often with Regency and Colonial elements, all built in the thirties and forties. Remodeling this kind of house to free new sources of light and space without disturbing the environment calls for ingenuity and archi-tectural diplomacy. When the owners asked architect Charles Tapley to design annexes for them, he changed the front of the house very little. Instead of front lawn, he put down a paved courtyard. Windows were extended to ground level—sober, tasteful adjustments. In the back, how-ever, everything takes off dramatically. A two-story gallery opens up all rooms, ex-tending space, flooding them with light, loosening up their functions. Off the old kitchen wing, another annex, shaped like a tiny amphitheater, encloses a children's play area. The center section of the gallery is a glass-walled double-story atrium, roofed with a skylight. Next to it the old library rises to the same height, its ceiling knocked out, bringing airiness into a formerly gloomy, oppressive room.

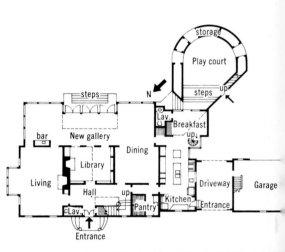

Glistening glass addition, top, behind the con-ventional Georgian red-brick façade, above. Sweeping curve, right, encloses playground and adds a second-story walkway. Adding the gallery gave all the old rooms a new look, as in the case of the library, opposite, now double-height.

Tinted glass and louvered shutters help to make the glass gallery cool in such a hot climate. This dramatic addition extends both living and dining rooms, which are now filled with light, plants, and potted trees. The atrium in between, rising two stories, brings sun across a ramp that runs between the owner's new office and the guest room and bath, and into the opened-up library. The renovation also added a new kitchen, indoor and outdoor play space for children, plus a bay window to the master bedroom. The children have easy access to their rooms via a bright green metal staircase spiraling up from the kitchen. They also have a new fire escape, incorporated into the curving wall of the amphitheater playground. Where once formality ruled the house, there is happy informality. When the family entertains now, they have space to set up a buffet on one table and seat everyone at a second large table. Modern furniture added to the traditional antiques helps to relax the living room. Just as indoors underwent changes, so did the back yard. Formal beds and a very precise lawn gave way to the original contours of the land where shallow ravines and mature shade trees with a variety of undergrowth reasserted a more natural order.

Skylight, opposite far left, brings sun into the two-story atrium. The room in back is a new office. Dining room with sun yellow walls, opposite, is now a big opened-up space with two tables. Big plus for the children: outdoor and indoor play areas off the new kitchen so the cook can be doing everything she needs to while keeping a watchful eye. Extra security for youngsters: the fire escape, opposite top, that rims the curving amphitheater wall.

EXCITING DOUBLE-DECKER WING

When a house begins to show its age and unadaptability to today's ways of life, it's time for a face-lift. Building on a new extension can remedy in one sweep a lot of shortcomings. Rarely, however, is an addition such an eye-grabbing contrast to the old as the playful architectural fantasy designed by architect Michael Graves for Dr. and Mrs. Paul Benacerraf's house in Princeton, New Jersey. An assembly of cutout white stucco panels and soaring col-

umns and beams, splashed with accents of bright yellow, blue, red, and green, the new wing, jaunty as a ship, juts out into the back garden, adding a breakfast room and a playroom for the couple's three children, plus a sunny deck on top. Seen from the street, the English Tudor–style house gives no hint of the surprise at its back. In contrast to the inward-turning quality of the old house, the new wing captures the outdoors. A curving wall of glass panels wraps around one side, letting in abundant light. The top deck is a high-flying super-structure of white posts and beams, girdled with white-painted railings. Just as on board ship, when you peer over the edge you look down on another deck wrapping around the lower level of the new wing. Not all the superstructure is there entirely for playfulness' sake. The stucco panels ward off some of the sun and together with beams throw patterns of shade across the deck floor, to create an ever-changing "painting" as the sun moves across the sky.

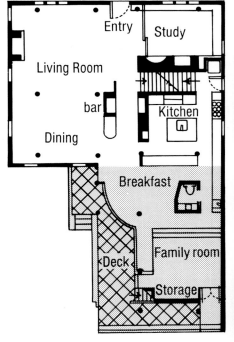

White stucco addition brings sunshine and nature into a gloomy Tudor-style house. This page, top left, the breakfast room with its garden view. From there it's just two steps down to the new playroom, bottom left, making it easy to keep in close touch with children from the kitchen. Lights are movable, clipped on chrome ceiling poles. Adding the new wing spurred other remodeling down-stairs. Living-room walls were replaced with steel posts and beams. The kitchen was entirely rebuilt around a center cooking island. The wing includes a mini-bathroom for quick cleanups before the children eat.

21

TWO-STORY LIVING ROOM ON A 20s HOUSE

When architect Harwood Taylor decided to graft a new living room onto his 1927 Houston house, it just had to be different. The great two-story-high sculptural space he designed splays out to a swath of glass 25 feet long, overlooking a new pool out back. He devoted half the ceiling to a sloping skylight of glare-free glass (great for lessening the load on air-conditioning, while allowing easy-on-the-eyes views of trees and sky). Also reflective, the glass becomes a mirror at night. Across the room, to hide the junction to the old living room, mirrors line two pull-to walls. More mirrors trim doorways, and a mirrored sculpture hangs in the window behind a room-width plant bed. The room sets up a counterpoint not only of mirrors but of curves as well, with its two super-embracing seating crescents in red leather from Italy. Outside, the old garage was torn down to make way for the pool, which is set on an angle to make room for parking the family's cars behind the mirrored fence.

Behind the traditional house, above right, stunning new addition incorporates living room, new kitchen, plus sauna. Curving stairway, below right, connects addition to upstairs rooms. Opposite: Living-room paintings by Dorothy Hood. In the back yard, top, mirrored fence doubles the yard visually.

NEW WING FOR WORK AND PLAY

After living in a vine-cloaked Georgian house in Houston for six years, Joan H. Fleming decided the family needed more rooms: a room for entertaining that could also be used by her teen-age sons, a home office for her business activities, a guest room and bath, a laundry–flower room, and a humidity-controlled wine closet. Since the only place to add space was at the back, architects Charles Tapley and Associate razed the old garage wing (cars now sit in a carport) and designed a wing that doubled the house. It extends the original structure back to the garden and a flagstoned terrace. The new wing, with an outside staircase to the guest room, is as contemporary as the street-side façade is Georgian. The contrast in styles was deliberate: vine-covered brick versus the simplicity of pine clapboard. Indoors, there is a beautiful interplay of ceiling heights: the contrast of one- and two-story-high spaces created by bridge areas on the second floor.

FIRST LEVEL

Laundry-flower room | Court
Lav.
Terrace | "New" room | wine
steps | closet
Gallery
Hall | Lav. | Kitchen
Living | N
Dining
Entrance

The new entertaining room, opposite and lower right, is part Boys' Town (they play bumper pool), part parental. All Flemings find it the perfect place to give a party. There is a bar on one wall, a stereo system on another, and people may dance on the gray-black terrazzo floor. The ceiling above zooms up two book-lined stories to sloping skylights. Upstairs, the new addition contains guest room and bath with open deck. The new home office, a businesslike complex of desk and files, occupies bridge space and flows into a flower-and-greenery-filled balcony, below left, above the garden, a pleasant place to work.

NEW WING WRAPPED AROUND AN OLD HOUSE

An old house, a new house—each distinctly itself, yet integrated, sharing the best features of both. "Here a door doesn't make an obvious difference between old and new," says Peter Saylor of Dagit/Saylor, the architects. They wrapped the new building around two sides of the old, extending the old roofline down in a simple saltbox shape. Front and rear, the addition respects the old style—in front, Colonial stone; in back, glass panels to go with the old small-paned windows—but on the side, a strong contemporary statement. The addition meets all the owners' concerns. They needed new and larger entertaining space, a guest room, study area, plus an opened-up master bedroom with new bath and dressing space. But not at the expense of spoiling the integrity of their cherished old house. Sympathetic design respected their inclinations, yet pitched the extension right into the twentieth century with its dramatic side façade (overleaf). Here an arched second-floor porch receives a diagonal outside staircase, creating a striking contemporary pattern.

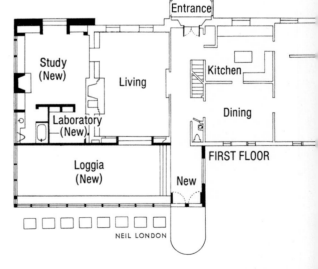

NEIL LONDON

Roof of the new wing is interrupted by a skylight and a small terrace outside the master bedroom, where dormer windows were lengthened into doors. In the old attic, a new bedroom, bath, and cedar closet are lit by circular skylights. The new loggia and entrance hall, opposite, extend living space for entertaining. The window wall frames the valley views beyond.

The end wall of the house reveals the vitality of modern architecture, with a stairway jutting down from the second-story porch for easy access to the pool outside. The shiny shaft of metal that carries smoke from the new study fireplace provides an axis for geometrical shape. Two rooms share the new space upstairs—master bath and dressing room. A sheet of glass tops the wall dividing the two to allow maximum light in both. The bathroom has a large tub planted squarely in front of a window. The house is so sheltered and the light so welcome that the owners have never felt the need for shades. Yellow ceiling maintains a sunlit feeling even on a cloudy day.

1: White mosaic floors the spacious bathroom and encloses the large tub and washing counter. 2: From the front façade, no hint of the new wing to be seen. 3: The end wall, white and modern in its arrangement of geometrical forms. 4: Peaked roof of addition from inside, showing glass partition wall which allows a flow of light. 5: Outside the master bedroom, a south-facing terrace is perfect for acquiring suntans.

1   2 3

4

5

SECOND FLOOR

Bath (New)

Study

Bedroom

Master

Dressing (New)

New

Bedroom

Balcony (New)

1 2 3 4

Dilapidated, derelict mill gutted and converted to a three-story house with winter and summer living rooms, and dining terraces down by the old mill stream.

Impossible one-room abandoned schoolhouse remodeled into a joyful little house for an entertaining couple.

Old Victorian firehouse recycled into a handsome living and working space for an innovative designer.

Flat-roofed, one-story cube house acquires a new geometry with gable-roof additions—extending space for a gregarious family.

4

5

Bath (New)

Study

Bedroom

Master

New

Dressing (New)

Bedroom

Balcony (New)

SECOND FLOOR

1 2 3 4

Dilapidated, derelict mill gutted and converted to a three-story house with winter and summer living rooms, and dining terraces down by the old mill stream.

Impossible one-room abandoned schoolhouse remodeled into a joyful little house for an entertaining couple.

Old Victorian firehouse recycled into a handsome living and working space for an innovative designer.

Flat-roofed, one-story cube house acquires a new geometry with gable-roof additions—extending space for a gregarious family.

5 6 7 8

An ordinary builder's house takes on new character with opened-up rooms, big panes of glass, and curving shingled walls.

Developing a talent for remodeling means learning to see the possibilities within the improbable. These five houses are all examples of such perception. Their rescue operations called for skillful adaptation of space, plus lots of imagination and energy.

INGENIOUS TRANS-FORMATIONS

GETAWAY HOUSE BY AN OLD MILL STREAM

Deep in apple country a hundred miles from New York, interior designer David Whitcomb has turned an old clapboard gristmill into a comfortable country house "where everyone's itinerary consists of doing exactly as he pleases." The mill was a disused tangle of old wood buildings when he found it. He stripped down the structure to a bare skeleton and proceeded to remodel it into a year-round escape haven. Apart from old beamed ceilings, you would hardly recognize the original mill. Local fieldstone has been used to make walls and terraces. French windows and balconies open up the new three-story house to light. The renovation has turned the old wheel room into a kitchen/dining room. Above this are two sitting rooms (one for winter, the other for summer) and, on the third floor, two bedrooms plus bath. It's a joyful house in winter, when fires are burning brightly and ice is on the stream, or summer, when everyone moves outdoors to enjoy the pleasures of shady trees and cool rushing water.

1: Terrace stretches to within a stepping-stone of the mill stream, where guests often sit for lunch with a centerpiece of buttercups, 2, on the table. At breakfast, everyone invades the lower-level dining room, 3, cum kitchen, 4. For lazy summer days, a hammock, 5, swings over the meadow grass filled with wild flowers. On another terrace, 6, chairs share the view with the old water wheel. Inset: Old mill before remodeling.

To open up the house for summer, Mr. Whitcomb added at the front, one long beamed room with deep bay windows and a cool tiled floor. This new wing is the mill's most frequented sitting place, he says, "the perfect spot to have cocktails and watch the humming-birds in the garden." Terra-cotta tiles here and on the kitchen floor have built-in drains, so he just hoses the surfaces clean. The living room upstairs (cozy with a fire in winter) is also a part-time study where the designer works at a writing table painted to resemble woven straw. The mill is furnished with a treasury of antiques, including a special quilt, seen on the living-room lamp table. This was given to Mr. Whitcomb by the wife of a stonemason who combed the countryside for field-stones so the mill's exterior walls could have a unified look. He matched part of an old stone wall standing in the wheel room—the only original wall left intact.

First Floor

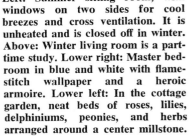

Second Floor

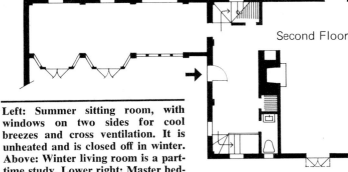

Third Floor

Left: Summer sitting room, with windows on two sides for cool breezes and cross ventilation. It is unheated and is closed off in winter. Above: Winter living room is a part-time study. Lower right: Master bedroom in blue and white with flame-stitch wallpaper and a heroic armoire. Lower left: In the cottage garden, neat beds of roses, lilies, delphiniums, peonies, and herbs arranged around a center millstone.

MADE-OVER LITTLE SCHOOLHOUSE THAT LIVES BIG

What do you do with an old, abandoned one-room schoolhouse that's full of mice, has a low ceiling and no water? If you are enterprising and enjoy taking up challenges, as Mr. and Mrs. John Dodds do (she's the stage and TV actress Vivian Vance), you buy it and find an architect who doesn't think you're crazy. Architect Harry Bates was the man who came to their rescue. "The schoolhouse couldn't possibly have been done without him," declares Mrs. Dodds. "It was nothing inside, but we didn't want to change the look outside. We could have added on, but Harry took an ax, broke through the ceiling, and crawled up into the hole he made and said he'd make us a whole house in the shell." So the structure was gutted, big windows put in the back, and a porch added at the side. Everything was painted white. Result: a perfect collaboration between owners and architect and a happy house.

Right: Renovated schoolhouse inside and out, spanking fresh in yellow and white. Big new windows bring in the light. Living room rises double height where the old schoolhouse ceiling has been knocked through. Mirror over the fireplace came from Tallulah Bankhead's apartment. Victorian chair from "I Love Lucy" set. Top: Before restoration.

Above: Mrs. Dodds relaxes in a corner of the living room, on the flower couch, right, which is below a book-lined balcony. "This house," she says, "is the easiest in the world to take care of."

Under the roof, in what was attic space (see plans opposite top), now reside the master bedroom and bath. The little round window in the bedroom, seen from outside, opposite lower left, is original to the old schoolhouse.

The house looks so small from outside that people wonder why Mr. and Mrs. Dodds bought it. Then they walk in and are surprised. "There's plenty of room," Mrs. Dodds says, "to entertain eighteen people in summer, with spillover onto the porch." Reached by a spiral stairway from the living room, the upstairs contains one bedroom, bath, and book-lined balcony plus five closets tucked under the eaves. With decorator Diane Russell, Mrs. Dodds chose easygoing fabrics in country chintz. All the slipcovers go into the wash. The carnation-print fabric in the bedroom is matched by wallpaper which then continues into the adjoining bathroom. "This is a joyous house, especially because we have only one bedroom and can't have sleep-over guests. Now all our friends want to give up their four-bedroom houses and duplicate this one!"

A VICTORIAN FIREHOUSE POLISHED AND BROUGHT UP TO DATE

Living in a firehouse, particularly one built in 1893, may seem like a trip to a distant shore of eccentricity, but to John Dickinson, a San Francisco designer of furniture and interiors, it is perfectly logical. He loves gingerbread architecture, and he knows how to combine the old and the new with distinct flair. In his firehouse, a second-floor space that was once the firemen's dormitory is now his living/dining/office, with no indication of where one activity stops and another begins. "I don't like static setups," he says. Since he likes to "shuffle things around," all electrical outlets are in the floor so he can have light wherever he wants it without tripping over extension wires. He works at a big art-nouveau table which is thought to have come from the French embassy in Vienna. The walls are as he found them, cracked old plaster the color of smoky topaz. He had them washed and touched up a bit and painted the old brown dado white.

Opposite and below: Living/dining/office in the converted firehouse. Designer Dickinson's drafting board and blueprint machine are built into storage by the windows. Stove in steel and brass with moldings to match the dado was designed by Mr. Dickinson, took two years to make. Firehouse, lower left, is ornately at ease on a stylish San Francisco street.

Everything that John Dickinson designs has a measure of whimsy, such as tables with animal legs, and lamps that look like porcelain mushrooms straight out of Alice in Wonderland. He delights in creating fool-the-eye furniture—pieces that seem to be made out of hand-hewn rock but turn out to be wood, or "rough-sawn" tables that prove to be plaster. He'll paint an old chest to look like tiles and use it brilliantly as a sofa table. Trompe-l'oeil trickery runs all through his firehouse, reaching its height in the dressing room, which resembles a little street lined with town houses; instead of doors on the clothes closets are replicas of Victorian façades, with mirrors for windows. "I drew it all up and a carpenter built it," he explains. The various sections all open out, with storage behind; shirts slip into slots like letters into a mailbox. In his bedroom, the four-poster has a "tiger" bamboo finish. The walls are covered with black vinyl that has a horsehair finish. The bath next door is set into a chassis painted to look like old railroad-station woodwork.

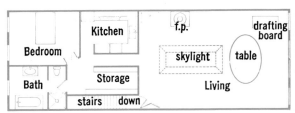

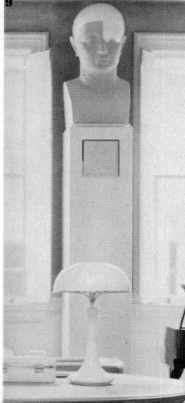

Finer points in the firehouse. 1: Art-nouveau oak table, stripped and waxed, seats ten. 2: Gray-flannel-color carpet has two borders, one white, the other brown. 3: Table that looks like rough-sawn wood is really plaster. 4: Dressing-room street façade carved in wood hides clothes storage. 5: Shirts and sweaters in their respective slots. 6: Chest table painted to look like tile. 7: Bertie the cat eats from a dish on a brass fold-up disk, as used on ships to climb to difficult places. 8: Kitchen paneled in white siding with brass hardware on stainless steel standard fixtures. 10: Plinth between windows contains handy storage and stereo speakers. Roman emperor on top is not marble but papier-mâché. 11: Bedroom papered in black vinyl, carpeted in dark brown. 12: Bath has a great mirror from an English pub.

New plan

Open
Bridge
dn
Dressing
Deck
Master | Guest

Loft
Daughter
NEW
SECOND
FLOOR

Deck

Carport | Court
Entrance →
Storage

Living Room

New entrance hall | open

New dining room

N

New study
Pergola
Breakfast
New guest room
New laundry
New family room
FIRST FLOOR "AFTER"

New kitchen
Terrace | Pool

Original house

N

Carport | Court
Entrance

Living
Kitchen | Dining

Laundry
Pergola
Master | Guest
Child
FIRST FLOOR BEFORE

A SMALL BOX OPENED INTO A FAMILY HOUSE

The point of any remodeling project is to create an environment to match a vision of the way you want to live. This house was originally a box: a nice box with big windows set four-square on an interesting piece of land. But for a gregarious family, it was very small. So architect Walter Ramberg started over: a new extension at the back for a family room, a steep-roofed second story over the original box for guest and master bedrooms, a two-story addition for dining and daughter's rooms. Inside, almost every right angle disappeared as spaces were opened up, heightened, stretched. Now, Mr. and Mrs. James Cutts have a house as varied as it is unpredictable. From the outside you can sometimes see completely through it. From the inside you catch tantalizing glimpses of other house angles, or you may see nothing but woods, carefully landscaped by Mr. Cutts to conceal the outside world almost completely.

Top and left: The original box (inset opposite) is in the center (with second-story gable-roof addition). The single-story extension contains new family room. Flat roof makes a deck for master bedroom. To right of picture is the gable-roof dining addition. Inset: The narrow bleached-redwood siding of the new addition gives the original living-room walls with old brick chimney the rustic warmth of a Vermont barn.

"It's a contemporary house but romantic," says Mrs. Cutts. "A setting for a creative family." In the new family room, a flokati carpet matches the nubbly texture of the woods and grass outdoors. An old family piano and two new sofas join an oak coffee table made by Mr. Cutts. Ann Cutts, an imaginative teen-ager, wanted stars painted on her bedroom ceiling—and she has them. Her room is almost double height, with an overhead play loft that floats under the peaked roof, accessible by a little red ladder from her sleeping area. The new entrance space to the house, says architect Walter Ramberg, "was an exercise in judicious extravagance." It is actually the largest space in the house and perfect for large-scale entertaining. All the service areas of the house are now pulled together in a spacious trapezoid that saves steps and allows the cook privacy or company as she chooses. The angled kitchen leads easily into the dining room. The breakfast corner opens to the pool in summer for alfresco food and drinks.

New family room, 1, was designed for comfort and light, with big windows looking onto the garden. 2: Daughter's loft for play over the sleeping area, 3. The room is reached by a bridge, 4, over the hallway. New entrance hall, 5 and 6, with the rich colors of an antique Soumak rug to warm a bluestone floor. Painting, like most in the house, is by Mr. Cutts. An old Japanese chest, stripped down, holds plants. Angled kitchen, 7, and breakfast corner, 8, are painted a strong parrot green.

4

7

8

5
6

A BUILDER'S HOUSE GETS TRANSFORMED

"Simplify, simplify," Thoreau advised, and this skillful remodeling does just that, combining small rooms into larger, replacing undersized separate windows with glass walls, and banishing everything fussy. Architect-owner John Bedenkapp has transformed what was once a builder's house into a place tailored to his personal needs—relaxation, hospitality, gardening,

and solitude. The original garage has been cleverly converted into his private wing, with master bedroom, bath, and study, reached by a covered brick-paved breezeway from the main building. His opened-up living room was enlarged by annexing the old front porch. Through a new expanse of glass, it looks onto a trellis-covered deck, added at the back of the house.

In the living room, right, walls and floor are white, the latter painted with six coats of deck enamel for a tough finish. Classic modern furniture by Mies van der Rohe creates a spare look. The stainless steel drum table is designed by Bedenkapp. On it, a collection of sixth-century-B.C. Corinthian pots. Through the window, the view is of terraced grassy steps, above left, going down to the woods.

The house before additions and remodeling

Terraced lawn sloping from the new dowel deck

"Remodeling is finding space you didn't know you had," says John Bedenkapp. For him, escape from the helter-skelter of city life means a house that is elegantly furnished yet uncluttered, and very quiet. His masterly revision of a commonplace house, which was very much the same as all its neighbors, doubles his living space. He now has two guest rooms upstairs and his own convenient retreat—a personal suite away from the house proper. Since he goes everywhere by bicycle in the country, the garage was just wasted space, so he converted it into a private haven. Cedar-shingled walls, decks, and a sheltered courtyard tie the two buildings into a unified whole. Except for green plants, the leathers and polished dark wood of furniture, and a few modern paintings, everything about the house seems to be either white or soft gray. The new openness everywhere brings the indoors closer to nature. From every room there are views of the outdoors—the day lily garden, the lawn and patio, the woods. Mr. Bedenkapp says he enjoys the winter scenes even more than summer—a tribute as much to his garden plan as to his architectural renovation. The hill that slopes down to the garden is stepped with railroad ties—an imaginative detail in a rich treasury of house and garden ideas.

The deck, made of dowels, shaded by a dowel trellis
Living room, incorporating a former front porch

Brick patio between house and separate master suite   The new library, once a small front parlor

In the living room, a skylit wall, another of clear glass. Floors are slick white paint
Once a garage, now a master bedroom-study retreat   From the master bedroom, a wide-angle view of the woods

1

Breaking through
an exterior wall to include
a porch and
terrace.

2

Creating an open
architectural
environment
from three
difficult rooms.

3

Traditional
apartment blown
apart into a
series of curving
spaces for easy
living.

4

Two rooms
merged into
one glistening,
totally space-
age environment.

5 6 7 8

he open-ended
ft look—
 walls to
utter the
ace or interrupt
e eye.

Making a clean sweep of space within a space: this is another aspect of remodeling. When walls are taken away, suddenly the whole perspective changes. Shown here, five interesting ways to explode the boxy boundaries that inhibit living.

ONE GREAT BIG BOUNTIFUL ROOM

It was just an ordinary little weekend and vacation frame house and the family wanted more space. So interior designer William Machado extended the ground floor by taking down an exterior wall and building out. This one great room incorporates what was once the old front porch and an adjacent terrace into the original existing living room. Although this makes a large space, there are nice cozy areas within it: the fireplace, a card table for games, and a corner for dining. White-oak flooring seemed to capture the easygoing spirit of the extended room, so Machado took it right up the walls, too. Sliding glass doors onto the garden open the addition to the outdoors, so there is lots of room for summer entertaining.

THE EVERYTHING ROOM

Right: New extension begins where the floor level changes and the beam swings across the ceiling. Skylights in the slanted roof let in the sun. Above: A marvelous mixture of textures —wicker, glove leather, linen—on the seating around the fireplace. Color comes in through Oriental rugs and a pile of pillows.

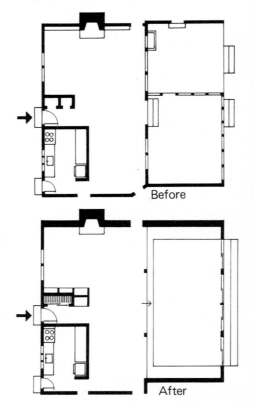

Before

After

Before

After

THREE INTO ONE FOR SUPER PARTIES

To make this space, architects Robert Mayers and John Schiff turned three rooms in the Bruce Slovins' apartment into one 60-by-16-foot environment. And within it they built another environment, a 38-foot structural unit in gray Formica which includes a hi-fi setup, love seat, bar, plus a multiplicity of tables all under a neon-lit canopy. "The flexibility of the space is fantastic," says Mrs. Slovin, an energetic and imaginative hostess. At maximum party potential, the unit becomes a banquet table that can seat twenty-five or serve a buffet for a hundred. A cube on one end of the unit opens on the diagonal and works as the bar. Extra panels that extend the structure for large-scale entertaining are stored on the wall as sculptural forms when not in use, leaving a permanent dining table for eight.

Opposite: Ready for a big dinner party, the unit seats sixteen. Dining chairs by Nicos Zographos are covered in the same rust leather as the armchairs, right, by Le Corbusier. Above: Mrs. Slovin prepares red snapper with tahini in the kitchen. This page, top: Mr. Slovin mixes drinks from the bar. Center: Plum-colored panel slides across to close off dining area after dinner.

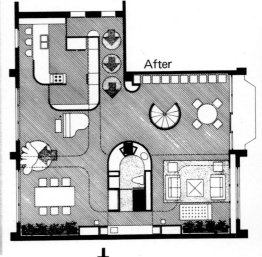

OPENING UP AND LIVING IN THE ROUND

This white fantasy was once a typical boxy two-bedroom apartment. The owners bought it and the identical apartment above and proceeded to have the entire duplex redesigned by architect Stanley Tigerman. With the bedrooms relegated to the second floor, the lower level was dramatically transformed to an open, flowing living space. Partition walls were ripped out and separation between spaces was made gentle with a series of curved forms. Easy maintenance was crucial, so walls were covered in either white vinyl or mirror, and built-in cabinets were surfaced in Formica. The new oak floor, laid interestingly on the diagonal, was kept for the most part bare and gleaming. Two semienclosed curved areas are the powder room and kitchen.

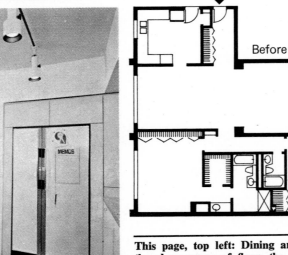

This page, top left: Dining area and, across the clean sweep of floor, the curved wall of the kitchen. Right: Sitting area, separated from dining corner by curved powder room. The floor-to-ceiling drum contains the spiral stairway to bedroom level. Center: Row of colorful padded cubes that move about the space for extra seating. Bottom left: Curving powder room. Right: Impeccably equipped kitchen. Above, center: New floor plan; below it, the original layout.

Above: Spiral staircase has oak treads and white painted metal handrail, curls up through a floor-to-ceiling drum lined with silvery Mylar. In the sitting area, windows are masked with plywood and wallboard pierced with round cutouts for light, creating a cozy niche for conversation. Other windows stretch from floor to ceiling and offer panoramic city views.

MAKING CURVES OUT OF BOXES

This wonderful room is in an old New York building but you'd never guess. It's been transformed from an old-fashioned, rather dark scene into a twenty-first-century setting. A partition was taken out, turning two rooms into one living room. For extra light, old casement windows were replaced by larger curved ones with gray glass and black frames. Four curved columns have been added to give an illusion of width and height in a long narrow space. The apartment is on a high floor, and the remodeling, in the words of designer Jay Specter, accentuates the feeling "of soaring in an airplane."

2

3

Above: Glistening white space with lacquered walls and marble floor; color comes in through art objects. White quilted Indian crewel covers sofa and chair. Steel and glass coffee table designed by Jay Specter. Top: No sharp-edged corners in this space-age environment. Windows have airplane curves. Door opens to curved steps which lead to a sheltered terrace. Right: Glass-topped dining table and classic French quilted chairs, a juxtaposition that gives this room distinctive character.

CLEAN-SWEEP SPACE FOR LIVING NOW

Though tempted to break up the 75-by-100-foot floor-through of an 1890s warehouse into smaller roooms, *Art Forum* publisher Charles Cowles realized that he wanted the experience of living in one enormous room where unobstructed space would offer almost Oriental serenity plus room for a growing collection of sculptures and paintings. Designer Mark Hampton helped achieve this spatial objective with a minimum of structural changes. A free-standing L-shaped wall sections off bedroom, library, and storage—and can be moved as often as the works of art, to suit the mood and the moment. Everything's painted white, the floor sanded and coated with a polyurethane finish. Hooked up gallery fashion, a system of track lighting illuminates a spectacular array of art by young painters John Clem Clarke, Llyn Foulkes, Nigel Hall, Robert Hudson, Tom Holland, Gary Kuehn, Ronnie Landfield, Jeffrey Lew, Peter Reginato, Ed Ruscha, Keith Sonnier, John Sweddle, William T. Williams.

Right and below: Cast-iron columns provide architectural elements in the vast, wide-open space. Opposite insets: Two bookcases mark off a study area; the bedroom, with drawer storage making headboard; kitchen has butcher-block counter that works for buffet parties.

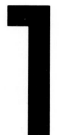 

Old plantation house
revived and given
a new double life
as a home for the
curators and a
museum for New Orleans.

Pennsylvania Dutch
farmhouse spreads
out its walls
and is filled with
magical craftsman-
ship, stencil patterns,
and painted floors.

Brick-by-brick
transplanting of a
Colonial house whose
gardens are now
as much in period
as the restored
interior.

Town house in
Savannah thrives
again with a galaxy
of modern color and
breakthrough in
planning.

5

d Texas farmhouse strides
to the future with a
w wing, terrace and
est house salvaged
om the old water tank.

6

Queen Anne manor house
on the Brandywine comes
to life through the
artistic efforts of two
very creative collectors.

7

8

Historical build-
ings don't have
to be turned into
museums. These six houses
are comfortable places for
thoroughly modern, down-
to-earth people who like to
live squarely in today—
with a sense of rooted heri-
tage.

RESTORATIONS AND REJUVE- NATIONS

OLD STONE FARMHOUSE WHERE TRADITION IS BROUGHT UP TO DATE

Superbly restored, this Bucks County landmark has recaptured the youth of a house that weathered the American Revolution (and much more) to find itself, over two centuries later, far handsomer than it ever has been. And more livable, too. The house was built in four stages, 1736, 1750, 1780, and 1961, when it was modernized and a new kitchen was put in. Interior designer–muralist Richard Neas, the present owner, calls the place Partridge Run. "Half the partridges in Pennsylvania seem to be hereabouts and they never leave." Mr. Neas loves comfort—and has it. He also loves the crafts and furniture of the eighteenth century. He has made the garden reflect history, too. It's a countrified parterre, with flower beds fringed in herbs. "Exceedingly practical. I cut both."

Below: Dining room that would have pleased William Penn, with original pine flooring, oxblood paint, Windsor chairs jacketed in a delightful gingham print. The table is set with slipware and Delft. Right: Geese cross the lawn. Right, below: The gravel/parterre garden and brick-paved terrace, all enclosed behind an oxblood-painted fence.

"Nothing in the world peps up an old house more than color," says Mr. Neas, who went to work with relish in restoring his farmhouse. The living room is furnished in pure eighteenth-century style except for the floor. This he painted "to look like a fantasy version of old rag carpeting." The guest bedroom is bright with flag red, white, and blue, with the bed snugly tucked away in a recess—a wonderful way of using an old Colonial device to keep warm as a means of making the room look more like a sitting room. Guest house, although new, is built in the style of early Pennsylvania architecture and makes a handsome addition to the property.

Left: Guest house, connected to main house by a gravel terrace. Below the fieldstone wall is the swimming pool. Top right: Blue and white bedroom in the main house, with original scrubbed wood floor, and Amish quilt. Below: Living room is cozied up with a log fire and Mr. Neas' hand-painted floor, needleworked pillows. Right: Guest-house bedroom.

"This poor old house was pretty wild when I came upon it," recalls Mr. Neas. "No one would ever have known it had been a very handsome wedding present in 1736." Where he added new rooms, he tried to make them look as old as the rest of the house. The kitchen, for example, is tacked onto the left side of the house and leads directly to the parterre garden. Traditional exterior siding of 12-inch board is painted oxblood red. Inside, there is a brick floor, and rough-hewn beams under a pitched roof. Even the nails that put everything together were handmade, Mr. Neas points out proudly. Cupboards are painted with the kinds of Pennsylvania Dutch designs found on old dower chests; the copper pots and pans on open shelves are really old. The kitchen is a nice place for supper, and in winter, when the spirit moves him, Mr. Neas cooks in the fireplace. Throughout the farmhouse, his creative genius is visible. The old log woodshed, for instance, became a "very workable mixture" of compartmented bath, bar, and flower room. Stenciling livens walls, doors, and floors. In the old days it was used if you didn't have enough rugs. "Today," Mr. Neas says, "we do it instead of rugs."

Top left: Rear of the old house before remodeling, and, above right, as it is today. The house is almost three times as large as it was in 1736. Right: The arbor that links the vegetable and flower gardens. Always blooming with grapes, wisteria, clematis, trumpet vine, or white roses to make a nonstop flower show. Below right: The guest room Mr. Neas calls the stencil room. He worked on the floor and then "didn't know where to stop." Stencils go over the fireplace and windows. Bed cover is an old Pennsylvania quilt, canopy made from a fabric copied from an old quilt. Below left: Decorative bathroom with wallboard walls painted in *faux bois* and then decorated with stencils. Mr. Neas made up the flower-and-ribbon design as he went along. Opposite: The new kitchen, quietly painted in antique gray but full of modern conveniences. Comfortable sofa and open hearth make this a place to sit and talk while the cook prepares the food.

COLONIAL HOUSE BECOMES A GIFT FOR THE FUTURE

Stripped of its grandeur, completely dismantled, a once proud eighteenth-century Maryland house sat in a crowded garage for five years before Mr. Leonard C. Crewe, Jr., came to its rescue. The Dr. David Ross house, built in 1749 in Bladensburg, near Washington, was razed in 1957 to make way for a highway. But all 22,000 bricks, the doors, windows, dormers, trim, flooring, paneling, and even the handmade nails were saved. It was architect Bryden B. Hyde who proposed that Mr. Crewe, instead of building a new house, restore, rebuild, and preserve this old house with 225 years of history, which in the War of 1812

had served as a hospital for both British and American soldiers. Renovation authenticity was assured through drawings, measurements, and photographs which had been taken before demolition by Mr. Hyde, as well as from records found in the Historic American Building Section at the Library of Congress.

1: As the house looked before demolition, and 2, as it is today, meticulously reconstructed on a hillside north of Baltimore, with a new wing added. 3: Daffodils from eighteenth-century bulbs. 4: Brick-floored porch, tumbling cascade outside.

A love of nature and beautiful things led Mr. Crewe to tend to the outdoors of his restoration as much as the indoors. The house is surrounded by trees and plants similar to those that were there in the eighteenth century, a joy to the eye in all seasons. Collections enrich the rooms. Staffordshire lines the recessed mantel in the graceful blue and white bedroom. The music room holds a set of Delft vessels, perhaps once used for storing herbs. In the dining room, the table is circled with a set of Kissing Parrot Queen Anne chairs. Just one nod to contemporary living: the old kitchen half below ground is now a winter party room—but party spirit may often be truly eighteenth-century, including bread baked in the old oven by the fire and lots of cider to drink.

1: Lacy hangings on the four-poster bed in the blue and white bedroom. 2: Flame-stitched chair in the cozy music room. 3: Queen Anne spirit in the octagonal dining room. 4: The front of the house viewed in the spring splendor from bulbs. 5: One month later, the approach framed by dogwood blossoms. 6: The original kitchen, or "keeping room," so named because a fire was always kept burning here. This room now is a center for winter parties.

4 5

6

1: In the dining alcove, English creamware made circa 1780 for the Dutch market, commemorating William IV. 2: The living room with original pine paneling and fireplace, and mostly Queen Anne furniture from Maryland, Virginia, and Pennsylvania. Door to the left leads to the "powdering room" where wigs were groomed. 3: Hillside daffodils specially chosen in England. 4: Back of the house with high-stepped porch. From the hill, a water cascade tumbles down into the swimming pool. 5: Old barn beams cross the ceiling in the new kitchen. The dimensional painted floor cloth was made by craftsmen in Annapolis. 6: A breakfast corner with a Welsh cupboard, gateleg table, and Windsor chairs made in New England.

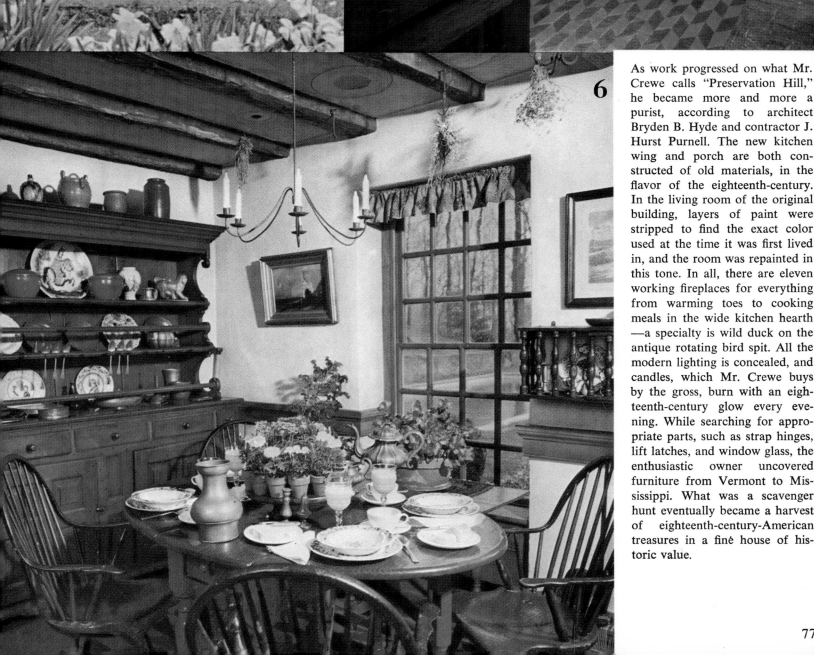

5

6

As work progressed on what Mr. Crewe calls "Preservation Hill," he became more and more a purist, according to architect Bryden B. Hyde and contractor J. Hurst Purnell. The new kitchen wing and porch are both constructed of old materials, in the flavor of the eighteenth-century. In the living room of the original building, layers of paint were stripped to find the exact color used at the time it was first lived in, and the room was repainted in this tone. In all, there are eleven working fireplaces for everything from warming toes to cooking meals in the wide kitchen hearth —a specialty is wild duck on the antique rotating bird spit. All the modern lighting is concealed, and candles, which Mr. Crewe buys by the gross, burn with an eighteenth-century glow every evening. While searching for appropriate parts, such as strap hinges, lift latches, and window glass, the enthusiastic owner uncovered furniture from Vermont to Mississippi. What was a scavenger hunt eventually became a harvest of eighteenth-century-American treasures in a fine house of historic value.

77

SOUTHERN GEM IS BOTH HOUSE AND MUSEUM

An antique gem on the fringe of New Orleans, Pitot House is a little mansion, once part of an old plantation, that now belongs to the Louisiana Landmarks Society. Not quite in mint condition, the house was offered to Mr. and Mrs. James Donald Didier as a residence if they would finish its restoration and be its curators. The Didiers had previously received honors for their interest in restoration, their town house in the French Quarter of New Orleans having received the Vieux Carré Commission's Award for Preservation. The Didiers couldn't resist the new challenge, so they moved in with their two children and most of their furniture and went to work. "We wanted a living organism," they explained, "not a tomb." They feel that historic houses should not be filled with the odor of sanctity but the fragrance of baking bread. Pitot House, consequently, is as alive as the day it was built. It is open to the public on Thursdays, and by appointment at other times for group tours.

Left: Study has renewed white plaster wall, putty green ceiling, brick floor, plus a portrait of James Pitot, a New Orleans mayor who lived in the house. Below: Upstairs gallery is shuttered in its original forest green. Carved figures are from the grand saloon of an old Mississippi side-wheeler. Greenery adds life. This page, top: Dining room with gondola chair and a punkah fan—eighteenth-century air-conditioner. Right, center: Children's room has pencil-post beds with fabric needlepointed by Mrs. Didier in *toile de Jouy.* Bottom right: Typical elegant mantel with a hearth of tiles.

With *his* antiquarian's passion for authenticity and *her* skill to reproduce eighteenth-century hangings, the Didiers brought the old Pitot House back to life brilliantly. Silk bed hangings and curtains in the master bedroom are designed in Federal style, all handworked by Mrs. Didier. Original wall colors were found by digging through an armor of old paint in every room. In the ground-floor paved gallery off the kitchen, shutters are forest green, set off with beautiful Venetian red for bow-topped double doors and window and the great beamed ceiling.

Right: Bedroom is a gentle contrast of the rich and simple. The old restored cypress floor is left almost bare. A Sheraton walnut chest with maple inlay stands below an ornate gilded mirror. Mahogany armoire is late eighteenth century. Below: Bedroom mantel is the rare Louisianan "boxed-in" type, hugs the chimney breast like a bracelet. Below: Grandest room in the house, the drawing room, also has the grandest mantel. Sheraton sofa and Louis XV table are original antiques.

Left and opposite page: The most picturesque room, used day and night, is a brick-paved gallery, open to the outdoors on one side. When the Didiers aren't entertaining, they like to prepare meals (enjoying the fruits of the garden) and dine at the drop-leaf table. Kitchen adjoins the space, through the double door.

BREAK-THROUGH IN A TOWN HOUSE IN SAVANNAH

"This town house looked great to us," recall the Charles Tallmans of their landmark house in downtown Savannah, built in 1848. "We moved here because it cost us ten dollars per square foot, as opposed to twenty dollars a square foot, plus the cost of the land, to build a house in the suburbs. We love its spaciousness, and the fact that our two boys can have the top floor to themselves." With no desire to do a purist restoration, the Tallmans were able to keep costs down, and because the house was built of wood, they got an effect with paint that "turned them on." Outside, it is the only plum-colored house in Savannah. Modern colors flow through their rooms, which is not surprising as Charles Tallman is a contemporary painter. "These houses get to be very expensive when you spend thousands of dollars recreating the precise molding that you have to strip off in order to rewire. I'd rather have a swimming pool in the back yard than moldings," admits Mrs. Tallman frankly. They stuck to a strict plan and resolved not to do things over and over, even though they might have wanted to. Their contractor was skilled at restorations, but the real secret of remodeling a historic house, say the Tallmans, is "knowing what you're doing before you start." They moved into the house at the same time men started work; they were finished in six months.

Opposite, top: The original house had three living rooms on the first floor. French doors separating this room from the middle one were taken down. Old church pews are used as chairs. One reason the Tallmans like these old, tall rooms is that they allow modern paintings to be hung without overwhelming the space. This page, top: Deep blue for the dining room, the third room on the first floor, to set off the Tallman canvas on the left. Old newel posts work as candleholders. Above left: In the boys' bathroom, a colorful effect with star-pattern wallpaper. Bedrooms on either side have white walls, ceilings and floors in different primaries. Above center: View from the second-floor deck, added by the Tallmans. The door—enlarged from a window—is to the guest room. Right: Looking out onto the deck, where Mr. Tallman painted an enlargement of a poster on the wall.

TEXAS FARMHOUSE RESTORED FOR A MODERN FAMILY

Cradled in the hill country of Texas, not far from the historic town of Fredericksburg, the George A. Hills' country retreat is a turn-of-the-century farmhouse so carefully restored and remodeled that there is very little evidence of where the old stops and the new begins. "This is a historical country," they maintain, "and we want a house that reflects its tradition." With three sons, they needed a lot of room, which they got with the help of design consultant Albert Keidel, a man with a passion for old local houses and the skill to update them with no loss of character. He complemented the limestone of the original farmhouse with board-and-batten exterior for the new wing, two materials as completely compatible as a friendly brace of country neighbors.

Left: New wing with sloping roof consists of one big room for living and dining, its east end devoted to quite a sizable open kitchen. A fireplace was carved into the limestone wall of the old house and works as an auxiliary broiler for Texas-size steaks. Furniture is a mixture of Victoriana and antiques of local workmanship, the rarest, a German-style armoire, made in the nineteenth century by Peter Tatsch. Next to it hangs a contemporary tapestry by hill-country artist Martha Mood.

Built with an eye to the breezes from the nearby hills, the Hills' farmhouse has a morning porch facing west, an afternoon porch looking east, and a north terrace for watching sunsets. Natural shade keeps the structure cool in the heat of summer. To extend the outdoor living, a large, sweeping terrace was laid of flagstone and river pebbles. "The boys helped us put it down," says Mrs. Hill. "Everyone pitched in as much as possible on this remodeling." The guest house is an ingenious bit of design. It was once the old water tank, a round stone structure topped by a cypress-wood tank. Replacing the tank now is a bedroom that looks like a toy chalet, reached from the lawn by a wooden stairway. The bathroom is below, in the cylindrical part of the structure, and has a deep, circular tub. Because all the new baths had to be fitted into nooks and crannies, tubs are all of mosaic tile and unconventionally shaped. "Once you learn how to fit into them, they're fine," says Mrs. Hill.

Far left: St. Augustine grass collars the geranium-dotted flagstone terrace circling the house. Beyond the lawn is a 50-acre wheat field where hummingbirds fly. 1: Guest-house bathroom with wooden baffle in back of tub made from recycled staves of the old water tank once overhead. 2: Guest house seen from the terrace. Stairs lead to bal-conied bedroom. 3 and 4: The Hills collect anything old and local. Chairs on the terrace are old plow seats. Barn siding is hung with an amusing frieze of road signs and other Texas memorabilia.

FOUR HUNDRED YEARS OF HISTORY TREATED WITH RESPECT

The house that Mr. and Mrs. George A. Weymouth restored and now live in is at the Big Bend of the Brandywine River in Pennsylvania. These same acres were sold to William Penn in 1683 by Seketarius, chief of the Lenni Lenape Indians. In 1763 Harry Gordon, a Scottish captain in the Royal Engineers, acquired the land and, using the old Indian trading post as a foundation, put up a manor house in the Queen Anne style. It was a summer retreat, an escape from the heat of Philadelphia. The house was almost derelict when the Weymouths bought it in 1961, but they have restored it faithfully. Built on sloping ground and cradled by ancient trees, it is four stories high on its river side, three on the other. Says Mr. Weymouth: "I can't bear a restored house with its beautiful old bones no longer showing. We imposed nothing on this. The bones show. We just added the furniture, and all of it is old." A painter, Mr. Weymouth is also president of the Brandywine Conservancy and a driving force behind the Brandywine River Museum. He painted *The Way Back*, right, when the house began to resemble its former self. The horse, Levi, was chosen as a model because of his willingness never to move if he could stand still.

Born and raised in the Brandywine Valley, both the Weymouths have grown up surrounded by old houses. They have been antique collectors for years and will go anywhere, any time, if they hear of a precious piece that has suddenly come on the market. They love beautiful old furniture, and if they can replace something good with something better, they do it. "When you restore a house, you must make the most of its character," they say. "There's no point in making it look new." Downstairs, in what was once the old summer kitchen, a brick-paved floor and beamed ceiling provide the framework for a wonderful live-in party dining room. To reach it, you go downstairs alongside a pierced stair rail acquired from an old Moravian farmhouse. The Weymouths changed the pitch of the old staircase to install the rail. The only dining table they thought right for this room belongs to the Metropolitan Museum, so they had it copied in old wood. Rush-seated ladderback chairs surround it. Seats around the fireplace at the other end of the room are all different. "They're like people," explains Mr. Weymouth. "They have too much character to come in pairs."

Above: The approach to the house is a country road that meanders through fields and meadows, then suddenly stops. The nearby rise is called Point Lookout; it was once a strategic site used by Indians.

Left: Moravian-farmhouse stairway leading down to live-in party dining room. Door in back is to the new kitchen. (Mrs. Weymouth believes in modern kitchens and baths.)

Below: Dining end of the raftered room. The still life is one of the few that N. C. Wyeth, Mrs. Weymouth's grandfather, ever painted. His wife called it "that picture with my eggplant in it."

Above: Baskets hang from the beams over the sitting end of the party dining room. Some are tiny, "for violets," and some are large enough for a summer picnic.

Near right: Behind the dining table, a beautiful old Delaware side cupboard is filled with Mocha and Bennington ware. The Weymouths set the dining table with slipware, pewter, dyed bone-handled cutlery, and iron candlesticks known as hogscrapers (which is what they were used for when not doing table duty). **Far right:** Over the fireplace, a spit called a clock jack still turns and roasts meat to perfection, like a non-electric rotisserie.

Left: The dining-room furniture is extraordinary Philadelphia Queen Anne. Walnut chairs have unusually high backs. Portrait of Mrs. Weymouth over the fireplace is by her father, John W. McCoy II. Below left: In a guest bedroom, a Hepplewhite bed wears a crocheted spiderweb canopy and is spread with an old Pennsylvania quilt. Below: Stair landing has two treasures, an arched window and a chandelier that kept up with progress by being converted from candles to whale oil.

The Weymouths insistently believe that "beautiful old things were made to be used." They reject the devout attitude of the collector who places precious objects behind vitrines, or fences off furniture with red velvet rope. "If a marvelous old chair has a case of the shakes, we have it fixed and then sit on it. That's what it was meant for. If you choose to live with old furniture, you must make friends with it, use it, and love it. But not, for heaven's sake, make it an untouchable." Since none of the rooms in the manor house is large, all the furniture is small in scale. "We didn't want the restoration to become all furniture and no house." Their love of antiques extends to horse carriages, which help maintain a continuity in their life style, indoors and out.

Canal engineer's cottage becomes a beautiful three-story fieldstone weekend house.

Uninspiring forties Spanish-style villa turns into a handsome contemporary living environment.

Two-room fishing shack is raised up in more ways than one to make a delightful, cozy, weekend hideaway.

Victorian mouse of a house gets a dramatic face-lift inside and out.

5 6 7 8

Bursting through a ceiling, extending one wall, and adding a rose-trellised deck change an ordinary three-room house into a charming cottage.

With effort and enthusiasm no remodeling project is really impossible. These five cases prove the point. Each house would probably have been abandoned by less imaginative owners.

THE HOPELESS LITTLE HOUSE

HOW TO BRING A HOUSE BACK TO THE LAND

Perched on a hill three hundred feet above the Delaware River and Canal in Pennsylvania was a onetime canal engineer's cottage built in 1827, set in 28 acres. When June and Jack Dunbar found the property, the house was pink stuccoed, with roses trailing around the Victorian porch. They wanted a weekend and vacation house and it seemed perfect. The first summer all the charm was there; then things began to get on their nerves. "There was no horizontal place on the land. We longed for a flat plane," they recall. Jack Dunbar, an interior designer, had the idea that the house should sit on a great platform. Fieldstone seemed right, because it was a locally available material. Before they knew it, major remodeling was underway. To build the terraces, which extend the living space tremendously, they had to take away the porch. To create more interior space, they turned the two-story cottage into a three-level house by dropping the soil line and carving out the basement. This space is now a kitchen/dining room with stone walls, a concrete floor, and doors opening onto a terrace for alfresco dining. "People say the house looks very Provençal, but actually we had never been to the south of France when we planned this renovation," says Jack Dunbar. "We were just trying to rescue a simple little house."

Rambling little cottage, left, before remodeling, and as it is today, opposite, a charming three-level house. Below: Tiers of terraces extend the living space. The Dunbars chipped off stucco from the original building, repointed the fieldstone beneath, putting yellow ocher in the gray mortar to give it a warmer glow. They hauled rocks from the surrounding meadows for the terraces, which they built themselves with the help of one man. Far left: The original detached kitchen became a studio bedroom; the passage between it and the house is now a new front entrance.

Typical of the houses along the old canal, the Dunbars' is quite small, 18 by 28 feet on the outside; stone walls 18 inches thick limit the interior space to just 15 by 25 feet. Putting the kitchen/dining room in the newly excavated basement helped them manipulate the total space to the best advantage. The main living room is on the ground floor, and over this the master bedroom and bath. The renovation disposed of the original stairway. In its place, Mr. Dunbar designed a spiral of pine treads, anchored in a telegraph pole. Three men took two days putting this wooden pillar into position. "Then," Mr. Dunbar says, "I discovered you can be just so poetic. People were afraid to use these stairs, so I had to design a rail." Using found objects was part of the Dunbars' plan. The dining table, for example, consists of two sawhorses supporting a piece of plywood found in the barn. This is covered with white plastic underlined with a flannel blanket. It looks like soft, white Formica.

Left: Living room is white and very light, with French casement fixtures and double doors replacing the old nine-on-six paned windows. It is sparely furnished because the Dunbars care more for art and plants than conventional furniture. By the rush sofa is an abstract by Nobu Fukui. Geometric opposite is by Robert Swain. Top right: The kitchen designed not to look like a kitchen. A gourmet cook, Mrs. Dunbar prepares food facing into the room behind a white-Formica-topped counter, whose pine panels came from the ceiling in the former detached kitchen. Sink, stove, and working surface are contained along its length. The refrigerator is in a closet in the wall behind, next to the base of the old fireplace. Oak cupboards on either side store food and dishes. Below: The dining table, a do-it-yourself project from various recycled elements. Right: The handmade stairway spirals all the way up to the third-level bedroom, which has a view to the terrace, below right.

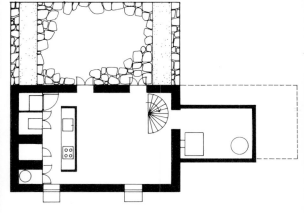

Above: Plan of lower-level kitchen/dining room, with access to a new fieldstone terrace.

Below: Plan of main living floor. New entrance is between house and detached kitchen, which is now a cozy studio-bedroom with its own private terrace.

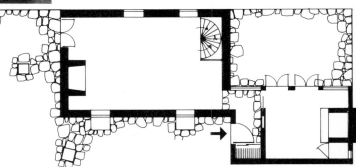

Wherever they could, the Dunbars opened the house to light and views. All shutters were taken off. Every nine-on-six window was replaced with a casement fixture and many new openings were created. Where wood window frames existed they were kept, and for continuity all additional windows were set in wood, too. It was part of the plan not to have any draperies or shades. The nearest neighbor is a quarter

Below: The tiny clapboard former kitchen takes on a new personality as a studio/guest room, lower left, with a trundle bed covered with Greek fabric and felt pillows. Walls, ceilings, and beams are painted white. The massive old fireplace makes a natural gathering point for art and plants. More plants line the passageway, lower picture, between the two buildings. Top left: Sunshine breakfast on the terrace which leads off the kitchen.

of a mile way, and "it's the kind of house you want to have open," explains Mrs. Dunbar. "Black windows at night don't seem hostile." The master bedroom went through tremendous transformation. Originally two small rooms with hardboard partitions between, it was dramatically opened up, a false ceiling stripped away, and timbered joists exposed. Closets divide the large space from a new adjoining bathroom. "Doing this house was like a Zen experience," conclude the Dunbars; "it nourished us both."

Above: Master bedroom with newly exposed timbers, a rich red rug on the floor. The Dunbars worked hard on all the neglected wood floors, using white oak, yellow pine, chestnut, and ash, whatever was at hand, for repairs. When the surfaces were restored, they were all stained to the same color and given a polyurethane finish. Mr. Dunbar experimented to achieve color uniformity, discovered that soft woods take the stain almost immediately but hard woods take much longer. Bedroom fireplace is plastered over, making a display piece for pre-Columbian art and contemporary African baskets. Center right: Baskets on the bedroom floor. Center left: Light well designed to bring more daylight into the kitchen. Bottom: Natural planting on the grassy slope going down to the old canal.

BIG SPACE IN A SMALL SPANISH-STYLE 40s HOUSE

A small Spanish-style 1940s house in Northern California—nothing remarkable, seen from the outside. But inside is an unexpected world of space, light, and purity of line. Space is created by taking everything out except the essentials. For the owners, Dr. and Mrs. Leo Keoshian, it's a nonmaintenance house. For the designer, John Dickinson, it's an understated house. "The trick is to eliminate rather than to add," he says. All the Mediterranean-style interior moldings and woodwork around the windows were replaced with fine modern stainless steel frames. This helps to give the room height. White blinds keep the glass free of clutter. The living room reflects shades of the white spectrum, infused with pearly light. A specially woven wool carpet with a Mondrianlike pattern in white, camel, and pale gray was designed to frame the location of the furniture. Canvas upholstery everywhere, with two sets of cushions (so one set is always clean). White vinyl bases for sofa, ottoman, and armless chairs. The clean white walls are outlined with dark wood trim at floor and ceiling and across the mantelpiece, giving perspective and contour.

Far left and top: White-walled living room, calm and serene with white-upholstered furniture, steel-framed windows. An old desk-table is an unexpected touch. Left: Two lamps have porcelain bases with baked-enamel shades, trimmed in brass. They sit on tables designed to conceal stereo speakers, brass-legged, with canvas flaps. The room and its furnishings were designed by John Dickinson.

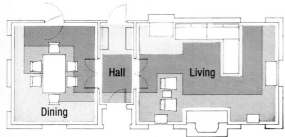

Hall   Living

Dining

The dining room in this little house of inventive ideas is in the same pale colors and beautiful materials as the living room. A white-lacquered dining table is matched with bleached-oak chairs adapted from a 1930s design, with white canvas cushions for comfort. Flanking the steel service doors are two consoles made of marble with a quarry edge. Above them are lighting panels, on dimmers and hinged like cabinets to facilitate changing the bulbs. In this remodeling, transformation is accomplished by means of good, pared-down decorating. Traditional Spanish touches such as the arched doors become handsome sculptures against white walls.

Above: Table setting matches the pure, uncluttered feeling of the room—a covey of white-china birds flutter around a centerpiece of unadorned bleached twigs.

Top and left: Arched entrances into living and dining rooms. Above: White canvas blind pulled down at window gives opalescence.

105

COZY HIDEAWAY FROM A TWO-ROOM FISHING SHACK

The location of a little two-room shack on the bank of a trout stream encouraged Mr. and Mrs. Harcourt Amory, Jr., to turn it into a weekend hideaway with the help of designer Nicholas Pentecost. First they raised the house fourteen inches off the ground, as it flooded easily when the river rose. To open up indoor space, they raised the roof and put in some old barn beams. A new plasterboard ceiling was given a coat of stippled sand paint and the joints were covered with barn siding battens. More barn timber created a dividing wall and counter between living room and kitchen and paneled kitchen walls. Picture windows replacing old six-on-six windows at the back of the house capture the river view. Then all around, black shutters on gleaming yellow-painted clapboard make a handsome finish. The Amorys furnished their "trout house" with English oak from an antique store they co-own in Bedford Village, New York.

Inset, top: Raising the house on concrete blocks to provide a new foundation. Center: The back of the house and the trout stream, the waterside ambience that inspired the remodeling. Right: The front gate, dated 1840, in bleached oak. Far right: Wedgwood fish molds mounted on a suede-backed board specially designed by Karl Springer.

Top: Living room looking into bedroom beyond, through arched doorway. Above: Kitchen alcove, with barn siding for a counter which has a butcher-block top. At the far end, original fireplace was boxed in, the chimney painted black. Far left: Fishing tackle hangs on barn siding which backs the refrigerator. Left: Tiny bedroom has Sun Valley quilt on the ceiling. Headboard is Elizabethan. The wheels come from a Scottish wool mill.

ADDING PERSONALITY TO A MOUSE OF A HOUSE

Never an architectural gem, this little house stood for a hundred years looking much as it did when it was built—until a few years ago, when it ceased being a mouse. In the course of twelve months a new wing was added, new plumbing, wiring, and heating installed; the entire exterior sheathed in gray-painted aluminum siding; and the interior ravages of time dispelled with the soft touch of the paintbrush, bright fabrics, simple, pleasant furniture. Ray Kohn, a floral designer and decorator who with Steven Derring is the co-owner of the house, knows just how to put a room together with expertise.

Above: Before remodeling, the front façade and side porch. Top: The house today, with addition of shutters, plus handsome new door and carved wood trim.

Above: In the living room, walls are hung with brown wrapping paper. Old floors needed nothing but scraping and a wash of white. The rugs are sisal, but Ray Kohn gave them borders of painted fringe to make them "feel like Persians." The brick-walled recess once held an archaic range (this was the old kitchen) and is now dressed up with a dais for a Franklin stove and a fern pot garden.

Top right: Stair hall has blue-lacquered walls, a pine table loaded with blue and white earthenware, and a Kohn arrangement of Queen Anne's lace—"Weeds but beautiful." **Above:** The library is the color of a lime except for a dado made of barn siding from an old shed. "It wasn't a very big shed so it's a very low dado." **Below:** Deck has a rush of wicker, plus two white benches, to which Kohn pulls up a long table for dining.

Left and above: New kitchen-dining wing paved wall-to-wall in brick-patterned white vinyl. The old trestle table is from England, the Spanish-looking chairs from nearer home, Sears Roebuck. Kohn hangs baskets as though they were paintings, and made the ceiling light out of a Japanese parasol. Instead of curtains, there are bamboo blinds and a drift of ivy over one window. A white-painted wicker tea cart is filled with ferns and potted flowers to "green up" the sliding glass doors that lead onto a new deck, right.

BIG LIVING IN A THREE-ROOM HOUSE

Before remodeling, this was a typical pleasant but tiny three-room weekend house, and patterned wallpaper and slipcovers didn't help its rather ordinary rooms. After—opened up and all white, a place where light plays all day—it seems like a big house. Its owner, Miki Denhof, has gained responsive space to live in, indoors and out, but the changes look more drastic than they really are. Rooms, roof, all but one wall remain the same. Redesign of windows in many shapes and sizes, asymmetrically placed to shape light and space, was critical to the scheme. With the help of designer Gina Beadle, Mrs. Denhof found that even a small house can have a surprising amount of space tucked away. Though there is no more room to live in than before, the psychological space-gain that occurred when the living-room ceiling was ripped down was very rewarding.

Above: Three rooms as they were. **Right:** Opening the ceiling to roof height in the living room expands the sense of space. Old ceiling joists are boxed in to form beams. Planks applied to strengthen roof. Indirect lights controlled by dimmers are mounted along the beams on the upper sides. The back wall in this room was moved out four feet to make a dining area and sliding doors put in to give access to a new deck. Plans, below, show house before and after remodeling. **Bottom:** Front of the house with its new door, wrought-iron railings removed, and new stairway. The exterior was improved with a fresh surface of bleached siding.

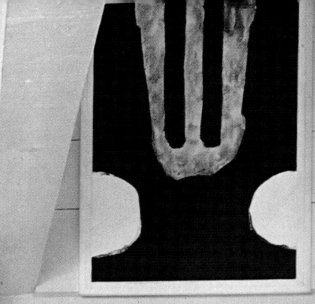

Above: Walls were stripped away from the fireplace to expose the chimney, which rises eccentrically to the middle of the roof. A wall section to right of fireplace was removed to admit light into a dark hall. Left side is surfaced with mirror cloth to reflect light from opposite window.

Above: Driftwood and Siamese rubbings make cabinet doors in the bookcase unit. Left: Hallway to bedroom. Below: Kitchen rejuvenated with fresh Formica surfaces and butcher block.

2

3

Above: In the living room, a high triangle of glass on a south-facing wall brings in sky and treetops and sunshine. A long slit, seen from the outside, below, in front of the desk throws light onto a white construction by Robert Courtright.

Crucial in this remodeling is the new deck, painted black to match the floors inside the house, extending living space out to the garden. Surrounded by thoughtfully sited trees, it has a bench built into the railing at one corner, herbs in a tub, white geraniums, roses everywhere. It fills the outdoor space between living room and bedroom, and both have glass doors opening onto it. On the outside of the house, bleached siding is overlapped more than usual to create the three-dimensional-line-drawing effect that Mrs. Denhof wanted. The interior is deliberately black and white with minimal touches of color, like the stenciled desk and bedroom fabric. Yet the atmosphere is gentle, softened by the trees, plants, and flowers all around. The house is *still* tiny, but almost nobody realizes it.

Above and below: In the bedroom, just big enough for two beds, two chairs, and a table for breakfast or tea, a sudden splash of blue, the only print and the only large area of color in the house. The daisy pattern adds fresh country charm. The horizontal windows frame greenery and provide cross ventilation.

1

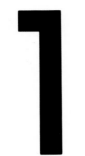

Circles and cutouts bring a modern feeling to walls of a sober Victorian house.

2

1 **2**

Cutting a dramatic rectangle in the roof makes an atrium in the center of converted stables.

3

1 **2**

Alternate stable conversion has a burst of plastic bubbles in the roof; exposed brick walls respect the spirit of the old building.

4

Graceful Georgetown residence assumes a totally different character at the back with modern extension.

5 6 7 8

In historic Savannah a three-level town house gets an interior remodeling and all the convenience of present-day comfort.

The scale of town houses gives them a very "human" quality. On the debit side, they often lack light and space. Here's how five town houses turned into wonderfully livable environments.

NEW LIFE FOR CITY HOUSES

OPENING UP AN 1880s HOUSE WITH ARCHES AND CIRCLES

Tall and narrow, this house in Georgetown had the grace of age, and a little of its internal awkwardness as well, when architect Warren Cox saw it. Over the front door was a fanlight, its shape echoed by a soaring arch in the living room. Mr. Cox picked up the theme, turning all the interior spaces into white modern environments, but relating architectural details to the original building. The doorway between the living room and library acquired a fan-shaped opening. A circle punched in the wall between hall and living room gives the old structure new dimension. This opening has a second function, holding a slide projector in a mirror box which throws images onto the wall over the living-room fireplace. The house is now a satisfying blend of old and new; typically, Rauschenberg joins Audubon on the new ledge for prints that encircles the living-room walls.

Top: Conventional red-brick Victorian exterior. Right: Modern furniture in the front living room, a cube coffee table lit from underneath, with a suspended light box matching it overhead. Below: Circular cutout in the living-room wall with slide projector for viewing pictures over the fireplace. Opposite: Looking from living-room arch to dining room through center library with new banquettes. Inset: Dining room from outside.

Right: Ceiling of the dining room is vaulted to continue the rhythm of curving shapes of old fanlights and arches. It floats free over the room suspended on rods from the old ceiling. Bulbs are recessed into this ingenious canopy, and light spills over the edges to wash the surrounding walls. Ceiling spotlights illuminate the tabletop from overhead; it was made by architect Warren Cox from an old door for this, his own house, and he used cane-seat Thonet chairs around it. The useful wall shelves for linens and silver were already in place. **Below:** Outside the Palladian-style doorway is a brick-paved outdoor terrace for alfresco drinks. Here yellow canvas directors' chairs and table are sheltered by an awning, and a gravel garden lies beyond. Above the terrace a second-story balcony is screened by latticework; the circular cutout repeats the house motif.

Architect Tigerman took nothing away from the original structure but added vertical cedar siding inside. He organized living on four levels, linked by a spiral staircase in a central shaft. All utilities are exposed. "Working on a budget, we had to hang these things out in the open." Ducts and pipes are painted Mondrian colors to distinguish their functions: blue for electricity, yellow for water, red for heating and cooling. For Dr. Christensen, a veterinarian full-time, musician part-time, the barn's lofty, cathedral-like proportions are a special joy. He plays the organ, located on the lowest level. Both he and his wife were brought up on farms, which makes barn living all the more appropriate for them. "We have a nostalgia for haylofts."

Opposite, far left: Frog Hollow barn poised beside the farmyard pond; inset, two members of the Christensen brigade, John and David. Left: Spiral stairway starts in the organ room and travels through four stories. This page, 1: Living room with comfortable modern leather chairs and a Franklin stove mounted on a marble platform. 2 and 3: Dining area, located beyond the kitchen, black Formica-topped table and cane chairs. 4: Kitchen gallery with open shelves for canned and bottled goods. Washer and dryer were set into storage wall. In back of this, dishwasher, range, sink, and working tops for meal preparation and cooking.

Master bedroom

Master bath

Boy's room

Children's bath

Bridge

Studio

Boy's room

Kitchen

Dining room

Living room

Storage

Organ room

Storage

For building material

turn to page 141

For painter Ann Christensen there is the special joy of having her own studio open to the house. It's on the third level, along with the two boys' rooms. "I can talk to anyone at any time. In my previous studios I always felt cut off and isolated," she says. What the family like most about the barn is the feeling that all the spaces are used. Architect Tigerman established color continuity with charcoal carpeting throughout—the Christensens like to walk about barefoot. All lights, including lots of bare bulbs and moon globes, are on dimmers.

Below, 1: Another glimpse of the living room with triangular window. 2: A boy's bedroom, with trundle bed for overnight guest. 3: *His* organ room. 4: *Her* painting studio. 5: Nature-watching bench beside a window, covered with carpet. 6: Master bedroom, with bath behind the headboard. Right: Central shaft, looking into a boy's room and living room below. Opposite, far right: Graphic windows open the black barn up to light.

The Christensen family, with their love of nature and animals, their closeness to growing things, and their innate visual sophistication, provoked Mr. Tigerman to make "as honest a response as I've ever made to any existing situation." The arrow graphic windows, for example, were determined by existing beams in the old barn—reinforcing the fundamental objective, which was to have a completely modern building that retains the *feeling* of an old barn. Asphalt shingles proved more economical than wood shakes. "We wanted to cover the barn uniformly because we like simplicity," explained the Christensens. "Using the shingles gave the barn a very dramatic effect, and of course they're so practical." It's like modern art, they conclude, in summing up their barn. "Such beauty in simplicity."

Left: An arrow of glass points down between two doorways in the barn wall. Below: Arrow lit from within by light. Christensen family sit on the nature-watching bench facing pond.

ACKNOWLEDGMENTS

A number of talented editors on *House & Garden*'s staff discovered and developed the original stories that inspired this book. In particular, contributions came from Will Mehlhorn, Elizabeth Sverbeyeff Byron, Jacqueline Gonnet, Babs Simpson, and Kaaren Parker. Several staff writers, in addition to Beverly Russell, produced the original copy—Kenneth Bates, Caroline Seebohm, Sandra Oddo, and Nancy McCarthy Richardson. This book represents recognition for everyone whose work has appeared recently in the magazine.

The photographs for this book were taken by Beadle, Emerick Bronson, Dean Brown, René Burri, Elliott Erwitt, John Hill, Marc Hispard, Richard Heimann, Horst, Robert Lautman, Fred Lyon, Maris-Semel, David Massey, Hans Namuth, and Tom Yee. The plans were drawn by Adolph Brotman, Neil London, and N. Siegel.